BookLife
freedom
Readers

AN OWL'S

LIFE CYCLE

BY MADELINE TYLER

BookLife
PUBLISHING

©2022
BookLife Publishing Ltd.
King's Lynn
Norfolk PE30 4LS

All rights reserved.
Printed in Poland.

A catalogue record for
this book is available from
the British Library.

ISBN: 978-1-80155-134-2

Written by:
Madeline Tyler

Edited by:
Kirsty Holmes

Designed by:
Danielle Rippengill

CONTENTS

PHOTO CREDITS

All images are courtesy of Shutterstock.com, unless otherwise specified. With thanks to Getty Images, Thinkstock Photo and iStockphoto. Front cover – Rosa Jay. 1 – Rosa Jay. 2 – duangnapa_b. 3 – Maksimilian, Toukung design, Rosa Jay. 4 – Africa Studio, ESB Professional, Aila Images. 5 – Anan Kaewkhammul. 6 – Mark Caunt. 7 – Vishnevskiy Vasily. 8 – PetraMenclovaCZ. 9 – Pictureguy. 10 – Kurit afshen. 11 – Mriya Wildlife. 12 – Gina Hendrick. 13 – Captivelight. 14 – Mriya Wildlife. 15 – Toppy Berry. 16 – duangnapa_b. 17 – Jim Cumming. 18 – BMJ. 19 – picturepartners. 20 & 21 – Maquiladora. 22 – Maksimilian, Florian Teodor, BIOphotos, Mr. JIRAKRIT SITTIWONG. 23 – ChameleonsEye.

WHAT IS A LIFE CYCLE?

All animals, plants and humans go through different stages of their life as they grow and change. This is called a life cycle.

 ➜ Adult

Baby ➜ Child ➜ Adult

WHAT IS AN OWL?

An owl is a type of bird. Owls have feathers, wings, long claws and sharp beaks. Owls have very good hearing and eyesight, which makes them good hunters.

EGGS

Female owls lay their eggs in nests. Many owls use nests that have been built and then left behind by other birds.

Nests are usually high up in trees, and owls lay between five and eight eggs in their nests. One egg is laid every three days. The group of eggs is called a clutch.

INCUBATION

After she has laid her eggs, the female owl sits on them to keep them warm. This is called incubation.

Incubation usually lasts for around 35 days. After this, the eggs begin to hatch in the same order that they were laid.

OWLETS

Young owls are called owlets. They use a special egg tooth to break the egg. When they first hatch, owlets are covered in tiny, fluffy feathers called down.

Owlet

Owlets cannot fly or find their own food. The father owl brings food back to the nest and the mother owl breaks it up for the owlets. Owls eat insects, fish and small mammals including mice.

FLEDGLINGS

When the owlets are about one month old, they begin to grow adult feathers. As they grow bigger, the owlets become fledglings. Fledglings are still small and still have some down.

The fledglings can now practise flying with their new feathers. Fledglings cannot fly very far because their wings are not fully grown.

OWLS

The fledglings become adults when they are fully grown and have all their feathers. They can now fly and hunt for their own food.

The owls leave their parents' nest to find a mate and a nest of their own. Most owls only ever have one mate. Soon, the female owl will be ready to lay her own eggs.

TYPES OF OWLS

There are over 200 different species of owl. Barn owls are very common all over the world and are found on almost every continent.

Barn owl

Snowy owl

Snowy owls live in very cold areas where there is a lot of snow. Their white feathers are a good camouflage because they are the same colour as snow.

OWL FACTS

Most owls are nocturnal. This means that they sleep during the daytime and come out at night to hunt their prey.

Owl Pellet

Owls often swallow their food whole. They cough up the bones and fur of their prey and spit it out as an owl pellet.

WORLD RECORD BREAKERS

Owls hold the record for the world's farthest head-spin. They can spin their heads the farthest of any animal – 270 degrees! This is almost all the way round!

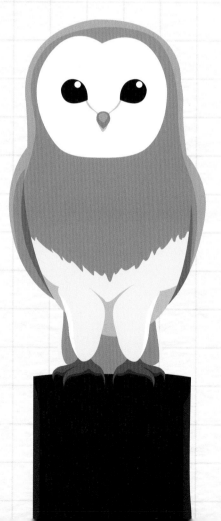

A man called Yaakov Chai set the world record for the largest collection of objects that look like owls. In 2016, the collection was made up of 19,100 owl objects.

LIFE CYCLE OF AN OWL

1 A female owl lays her eggs in another bird's abandoned nest.

2 The owl incubates her eggs until they hatch. They come out covered in down.

4 The adult owls leave their parents to find a mate and a new nest.

3 The owlets grow feathers and become fledglings.

Have you ever seen an owl in your local area? Visit a zoo or a bird sanctuary to learn more about different types of owls.

QUESTIONS

1 What is a group of eggs called?

2 When do owls hunt for food?

3 What are owlets' tiny feathers called?
a) Up
b) Down
c) Sideways

4 What are owls called when they start to grow feathers?

5 What does incubation mean?

BookLife
freedom
Readers